50 Great Reproducible Writing Workouts

Awesome Activity Sheets to Build Skills in Grammar, Usage, and Mechanics

By Stephen Krensky

SCHOLASTIC
PROFESSIONAL BOOKS

New York • Toronto • London • Auckland • Sydney • Mexico City • New Delhi • Hong Kong

Dedication

For Joan
—who punctuates my life perfectly.

Edited by Barbara Burt

Cover design by Jaime Lucero

Cover and interior illustrations by Rick Brown

Interior design by Ellen Matlach Hassell
for Boultinghouse & Boultinghouse, Inc.

ISBN 0-590-98408-X

Printed in the U.S.A.

Contents

Usage

Style

Introduction

*What is written without effort
is . . . read without pleasure.*
—Samuel Johnson

The Emperor Charlemagne, who took the throne in A.D. 800, was both a famous leader and soldier. But one of his most significant contributions took place far from any banquet or battlefield. A strong believer in education and learning, Charlemagne employed many scribes to make books. Without printing presses, however, the creation of even one book was an ambitious task. In addition, parchment was expensive. Whether from tradition or just to save room, words were butted up right against one another. That is, until the day when an anonymous scribe got the idea of putting spaces between them.

The idea caught on and, as a result, reading became more enjoyable. It had nothing to do with the quality of the writing; the books were simply easier to read. Just as this scribe clarified writing with one simple step, students can become stronger writers by developing a solid foundation of skills.

The ability to communicate well is a powerful tool. Within the writing process itself, there are smaller components that contribute to this clarity. Often it is the unheralded nuts and bolts—such as grammar, spelling, and mechanics—that hold the big ideas together.

This activity book is meant to give children practice in tightening those "nuts and bolts" of writing and to help students cultivate their own sense of style. The lessons are designed to develop basic skills with a sense of fun. By engaging their attention and imagination, we stand a better chance of teaching students to become competent and enthusiastic writers.

How to Use This Book

Welcome to *50 Great Reproducible Writing Workouts*! The exercises in this book are divided into six sections, starting with basic capitalization and punctuation rules and moving to aspects of style. Each reproducible worksheet begins with a simple explanation of a particular skill, such as using commas or fixing run-on sentences. The exercises in this book are perfect for individualized study. If a student has not mastered a skill already covered in class, the worksheets can provide practice. In addition, they can be given to an accelerated writer who is ready to develop more advanced skills.

If you are introducing a skill to your class, you can also use the worksheet as the basis for a mini-lesson. Start by reading aloud the Golden Rule in the box at the top of each page. In many exercises, an example is included to show how the skill is used. Following the model provided, prepare a few more examples to show students before they begin the exercise. You may ask them to work on their own or cooperatively in pairs or small groups.

Some suggestions for effective cooperative learning:

✎ In advance, plan partners or small groups that work well together.

✎ Ask students to take turns answering questions and explaining their answers to group members.

✎ Assign a task (such as quiet reading or writing) to be done when the exercise is finished. You can also ask students to work on the Extra activity at the bottom of each worksheet. This will ensure that groups that are finished do not disturb those still working.

EXTRA Activities

You will find an extension activity at the bottom of each reproducible page. These quick activities reinforce the skills covered on each worksheet. Have fun adapting these activities for your class and coming up with your own.

Name _____ Date _____

Always capitalize the first letters of the names of people or other characters.
This is true of first *and* last names.

Capital Crime

Find the names and circle each letter that should
be capitalized. You should find 22 missing capital
letters in all.

mother goose stood up before the crowd.

"Simmer down there, tom thumb. And you,
too, bo peep."

The pigs and sheep continued to mill around.

"As you know," mother goose continued, "someone
has stolen the capital letters from our names."

"I knew something was wrong," said chicken little.

"Stay calm," said peter piper.

"That's right," said mother goose. "I'm sure we will
get our letters back."

"How long will it take?" asked humpty dumpty.

"I hope it won't take too long," said miss muffet.

jack and jill nodded.

"Are there any suspects?" asked the Big Bad Wolf,
as he put something in his pocket.

"Not yet," said mother goose, clucking. "But I bet you didn't
know that I used to be a private investigator. I'll have this solved
in no time, and then we'll write a nursery rhyme about it."

Who do you think is the thief? <u>The Big Bad Wolf</u>

EXTRA Write a nursery rhyme describing what happens next. How do they
find the thief and who is it? Include as many characters as you can
and capitalize all names.

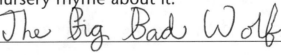

Name _____ Date _____

Lost in Place

Find the street names and circle each letter that should be capitalized. Can you find all 24 missing capitals?

"You're lost," I told my father.

"I'm not lost," he snapped. "Just a little, um, misplaced."

"Maybe we should ask for directions."

"Don't panic. We can retrace our steps. Let's see. . . . We came off the highway and passed graham road and elden circle. Then we took a right on main street, a left on midtown avenue, followed by a quick right on apple tree lane until it turned into macintosh circle."

"Uh-oh," I said. "I think we were supposed to go left on apple tree lane and then left again on trotting horse drive."

My father hesitated. "What if we keep going straight?"

I looked at the map. "It's a dead end."

"All right," he said. "Then we should go back to the intersection of apple tree lane and midtown avenue."

"Maybe we should stop at a gas station to ask for directions."

"No, never!" my dad exclaimed. "I know exactly where I am. And don't worry. I'll get you to the party before it ends."

⚬⚬⚬⚬⚬⚬⚬⚬⚬⚬⚬⚬⚬⚬⚬⚬⚬⚬⚬⚬⚬⚬⚬⚬⚬⚬⚬⚬⚬⚬⚬⚬⚬⚬⚬⚬⚬⚬⚬

EXTRA Write directions telling how to get from your house to school, or from school to your favorite place. Include at least ten street names and make sure they are capitalized properly.

GOLDEN RULE

Always capitalize the complete names of cities and states, except for little words like *of*, *the*, or *by*, as in the *District of Columbia* or *Manchester by the Sea*.

Capital Capitals

Find the names of cities and states and circle each letter that should be capitalized. There will be 26 in all.

Brian was pacing back and forth in his room. His mother was standing in the doorway.

"I hate tests on state capitals!" he shouted.

"Of course you do," said his mother. "Now, what's next?"

"oklahoma has the right idea," said Brian. "oklahoma city. It's easy. Why can't they all be like that? kansas has a kansas city, but they wasted it and used topeka instead."

His mother smiled.

"At least people should make up their minds about the kind of city they want." Brian shook his head. "I mean, look at boston, massachusetts, or atlanta, georgia, or des moines, iowa. Each is the biggest city in its state. But is that a rule? No. In illinois, it's springfield, not chicago. In washington, it's olympia, not seattle. In pennsylvania, they have two big cities, philadelphia and pittsburgh—and they picked harrisburg instead."

"You know," said his mother, "you're doing very well."

Brian shrugged. "Maybe," he admitted. "If I get an A on my test, can we go to honolulu? It's the state capital of hawaii!"

EXTRA List the ten cities (with their states or countries) you would most like to visit in the world and what you would do in each one.

Name _____ Date _____

ᘛᓂᘓᓄᘛᘊᓇᘈᘓ ᘊᘛᘊᓄᘛᘈᘊ **GOLDEN RULE** ᘓᘊᘈᘊᘛᘈᘊᘈᘈᘛᘈᘈᘊᘓ

Always capitalize the complete names of countries, except for little words like *of, the,* or *by,* as in *New Zealand* or *the United States of America.*

Travel Journal

Find the names of countries and circle each letter that should be capitalized. You should find 22 missing capital letters in all.

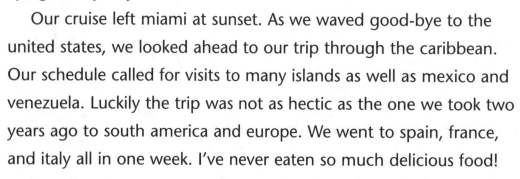

What a trip this has been so far! First, we flew to miami, after stopping off in new york to change planes. The ride was a little bumpy, but not as bad as the one we took last year to chicago. I still remember how my lunch went flying off my tray.

Our cruise left miami at sunset. As we waved good-bye to the united states, we looked ahead to our trip through the caribbean. Our schedule called for visits to many islands as well as mexico and venezuela. Luckily the trip was not as hectic as the one we took two years ago to south america and europe. We went to spain, france, and italy all in one week. I've never eaten so much delicious food!

Two days later we stopped in puerto rico. From there we sailed on to barbados and jamaica. The seas were rough on the first night. Almost everyone was seasick after the all-you-could-eat buffet. Luckily, I was so tired from playing shuffleboard all day that I slept right through the stormy weather. Now the sky is clear and the sea is smooth as glass as we make our way back to the united states.

ᘛᓂᘓᓄᘛᘊᓇᘈᘓᘊᓄᘛᘈᘊᘈᓇᘈᘓᘊᘈᘊᘓᘊᓄᘈᓂᓇᘛᘈᘊᘓᘛᘊᘈᘈᘛᘈᘈᘊᘓ

EXTRA Write a brochure for a cruise ship, describing all of its stops on a world tour. Be creative and think of some enticing features that would lure passengers onto your ship. Check your capitalization of countries and cities.

Name _____ Date _____

Always capitalize the first and last words in a title, as well as all important words (nouns, pronouns, adjectives, adverbs, and verbs). Little words like *a, an, the, of, at,* or *in* are capitalized only if they are the first or last word of the title. *Life on the Mississippi, Charlotte's Web, The Secret Garden,* and *The Great Brain Does It Again* are all capitalized properly. (Note that *It* is capitalized because it is a pronoun.)

Title Search

The entry below includes the titles of eight books. However, none of the titles include capital letters. Rewrite each title, capitalized properly, on the lines at the bottom.

"May I help you girls?" asked the librarian.

Ashley, Laura, and Julia nodded.

"We're looking for mysteries," said Ashley. "We just finished *the frog croaks at midnight* and *missing notes of the rubber band.*"

"They were a little scary," said Laura, "but not as bad as that math one—*stealing base 5.*"

Julia shivered. "I remember that one. But what about *the vanishing varnish*? Or *eyes of the potato*?"

"My favorite was *the rise and fall of argyle socks,*" said Ashley. "It was better than *birds of a feather in the heather.*"

"I figured out the ending to that one," said Laura. "Now the end of *out of air at the balloon factory* was surprising."

The librarian smiled. "You girls have certainly read a lot," she said. "Maybe you should consider writing your own mysteries!"

_____

_____

_____

_____

_____

_____

ᑫᖪᖱᕼᑫᕼᓄᕼᑫᖪᓄᑫᕼᓄᑫᖪᓄᑫᕼᓄᑫᖪᓄᑫᕼᓄ

EXTRA Write the titles of ten books you might write some day. Then switch with a classmate to check each other's capitalization.

Name _____ Date _____

ᖶᖷᖴ GOLDEN RULE ᖷᖴᖶ

Always capitalize the proper names of people, places, and things (including the
names of languages), as well as book titles and the beginnings of sentences.

CD-ROAM

**Find and circle the 55 letters that
should be capitalized.**

"what's that?" i asked at the

computer store.

"a miracle," said the salesman. he

held up a set of shiny cd-roms. "i have

here the complete phone books of

every country in the world."

"you're kidding! what's it called?"

"the only phone book you'll ever need. every

continent—asia, africa, north america, south

america, europe, and australia—is included."

"what about antarctica?"

"sorry. there are no phone books there, but we've got everything

from timbuktu to kalamazoo, from kuala lumpur to the house next

door. what do you think?"

"that really is amazing. i'm surprised it's all in english, though."

the salesman hesitated. "did i say that? there's certainly a lot in

english, but there are other languages, too. i don't suppose you speak

swahili, french, or thai?"

"sorry," i said. "i don't know all those languages yet. when i learn

them, i'll be back."

Name _____ Date _____

꧁ GOLDEN RULE ꧂

To show that someone is speaking, always surround the speaker's words—called *dialogue*—with **quotation marks** (" "). Quotation marks go outside any punctuation marks, such as commas or periods, that are part of the dialogue.

No Secrets

Read the selection below and add the missing quotation marks where they are needed. You'll need to add 24 quotation marks.

"Okay, we're all here," said Amanda. "Now what are we supposed to talk about?"

She looked around the clubhouse.

Mariel just shook her head.

Peter rubbed his chin.

"Come on," said Mariel. "Somebody must have an idea."

"I used up all my ideas yesterday," said Scott.

"On what?" asked Mariel.

Scott looked embarrassed. "I don't remember, but they're gone now. That's for sure."

Peter smiled. "I know why this is so hard," he said. "It's because this is a secret meeting."

"So?" said Mariel.

"Well," Peter went on, "whatever happens at a secret meeting is a secret, so that's why we don't know."

Mariel rolled her eyes. "But we're the ones having the meeting! If we don't know the reason, who will?"

Peter shrugged. "That's why it's such a good secret," he explained.

GOLDEN RULE

To show that someone is speaking, always surround the speaker's words—called **dialogue**—with quotation marks (" "). Quotation marks go outside any punctuation marks, such as commas or periods, that are part of the dialogue. Sometimes the dialogue is linked to a phrase identifying the speaker. At other times, though, the dialogue stands alone.

The Big Mess

Read the selection below and add 24 missing quotation marks where they are needed.

Look at this room! my father gasped. It's a mess.

I looked around. The room seemed fine to me.

I know where everything is, I told him.

My dad folded his arms. How can you say that? Your desk is covered with papers. . . .

Important papers, I insisted.

How can you find anything there?

I have my own system. It's, um, complicated.

Dad was not impressed. And the floor is covered with dirty laundry!

I was planning to sort it.

He laughed. In what century? And what about your bed? It's a wonder you don't hurt yourself on all the toys.

I think you're overreacting.

He shook his head. I don't. I would say a bomb hit this place, except then I'd see a crater or something. Now I want you to clean this all this up. Okay?

I nodded but didn't reply. Sometimes parents can be tough.

EXTRA Write a dialogue that takes place in a car. Use as many different end marks as you can (periods, question marks, and exclamation points). Be sure to put quotation marks in the correct places. It can be fun to share these aloud with students reading different parts.

Name _____ Date _____

Use a *comma* (,) to show a pause of thought or to separate connected ideas. Commas can also separate items in a list. But beware! Too many commas make a piece of writing seem choppy.

Touring the Zoo

The commas have been left out in the passage below, leaving boxes where they should go. However, there are also extra boxes where commas are not needed. Read the passage and put commas only in the spaces where you think they belong.

Welcome to the City Zoo! We ask that you listen closely☐ to the following description☐ which we will try to keep brief. To your left☐ is our Primate Habitat☐ home of our monkeys☐ chimpanzees☐ orangutans☐ and gorillas. Straight ahead is the Reptile House. This is where our snakes☐ alligators☐ and various lizards wriggle and squirm about.

Beyond the Reptile House☐ is our savannah and jungle landscape. Here you will find lions☐ tigers☐ antelopes☐ and elephants. We keep them separated so that everyone stays happy. We also invite you to visit our bird sanctuary. Our curators☐ have gathered birds from all over the world. We have everything from kakapos☐ to egrets. If you have any questions☐ please don't hesitate to ask. Enjoy your visit and remember that while you watch the animals☐ the animals☐ are also watching you!

⌇⌇⌇⌇⌇⌇⌇⌇⌇⌇⌇⌇⌇⌇⌇⌇⌇⌇⌇⌇⌇⌇⌇⌇⌇⌇⌇⌇⌇⌇

EXTRA In this zoo, groups of different animals like to do some of the same activities. Following the example, make up five of your own sentences. For example, *The monkeys, cheetahs, and polar bears like to throw popcorn at the visitors.*

Name _____ Date _____

Use a **period** (.) to mark the end of a sentence. Use a **comma** (,) to indicate
a pause of thought or to separate connected ideas or objects.

Stranded

In the passage below, the commas and periods
have been left out. Fill in each space with either
a comma or a period. You'll end up with 10 of
one symbol and 12 of the other.

When the spaceship crash-landed on the planet☐ its
captain knew his crew was in trouble☐ This sector was
outside the usual travel lanes☐ and they were there only
because the gravitational pull of a black hole had pulled
them off course☐

"Not too much damage to the ship☐ Captain☐"
reported the chief engineer☐ "Life support is holding☐
and the hull suffered only minor cuts and bruises☐"

The captain looked surprised☐ "Well☐ let's prepare
to leave☐"

"I was afraid you'd say that☐" said the chief engineer☐
"Unfortunately☐ the engines are off-line☐ We could be here
for a long time if no one answers our distress call☐"

"In that case☐" said the captain☐ "I'll have a chance to
catch up on my reading☐ Carry on☐"

The captain opened his favorite science fiction book, *Lost in
Space for Eternity*☐ The chief engineer wondered how he could
read a book like that at a time like this.

ᖬᖬᖬᖬᖬᖬᖬᖬᖬᖬᖬᖬᖬᖬᖬᖬᖬᖬᖬᖬᖬᖬᖬᖬᖬᖬᖬᖬᖬᖬ

EXTRA When one person refers to another person by name in a dialogue,
the name is separated from the rest of the sentence by a comma.

For example: *"How are you, Hilda?" asked Freddie.*
               "Freddie, I am just fine," Hilda replied.

Write a dialogue in which both speakers refer to each other by name
in every sentence.

Name _____ Date _____

GOLDEN RULE

Use a *period* (.) to mark the end of a sentence. Use a *question mark* (?) to show the end of a question. You can use an *exclamation point* (!) to show special excitement or action.

The Mad Scientist

Decide whether each sentence needs a period, a question mark, or an exclamation point.

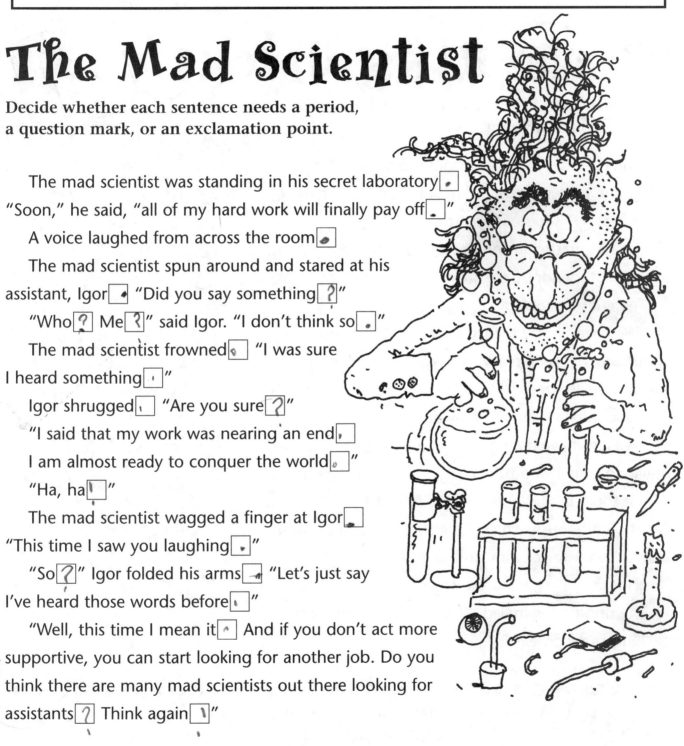

The mad scientist was standing in his secret laboratory[.]

"Soon," he said, "all of my hard work will finally pay off[.]"

A voice laughed from across the room[.]

The mad scientist spun around and stared at his assistant, Igor[.] "Did you say something[?]"

"Who[?] Me[?]" said Igor. "I don't think so[.]"

The mad scientist frowned[.] "I was sure I heard something[.]"

Igor shrugged[.] "Are you sure[?]"

"I said that my work was nearing an end[.] I am almost ready to conquer the world[.]"

"Ha, ha[!]"

The mad scientist wagged a finger at Igor[.] "This time I saw you laughing[.]"

"So[?]" Igor folded his arms[.] "Let's just say I've heard those words before[.]"

"Well, this time I mean it[!] And if you don't act more supportive, you can start looking for another job. Do you think there are many mad scientists out there looking for assistants[?] Think again[!]"

EXTRA Write a dialogue in which someone is asking you questions and you have all the answers.

50 Great Reproducible Writing Workouts Scholastic Professional Books

17

Name _____   Date _____

GOLDEN RULE

Use a *period* (.) to mark the end of a sentence. Use a *question mark* (?) to show the end of a question. You can use an *exclamation point* (!) to show special excitement or action.

Three-Ring Circus

Fill in each space with either a period, a question mark, or an exclamation point.

"Ladies and gentlemen," said the ringmaster, "welcome to our circus[!] Are you glad to be here[?]"

"Yessss[!]" shouted the crowd[.]

The ringmaster smiled broadly[.] "We have brought together stupendous acts from all over the world[!]"

The crowd cheered.

"We have Shorty the Lion Tamer," the ringmaster continued[.] "Is he really as brave as you think[?] You will be amazed[!]"

"Oooooh[!]" said the crowd[.]

"We also have daring men and women who defy gravity on the flying trapeze[!] But will they be able to defy it tonight[.] Who knows[?] And last, we have the Great Blunderbuss, who will be shot out of a cannon[.] Do you want to see him land on the moon[?]"

"Hooray[!]" cheered the crowd.

The ringmaster smiled. "Get ready for the most exciting show on earth[!]"

EXTRA

Write a conversation among three people. Use different end marks to express the following about each character:

• Jerry is always bubbling over with enthusiasm.
• Terry is constantly questioning everyone.
• Kerry never shows emotion and never asks any questions.

Name _____ Date _____

ᑫᑲᕐᕊᑫᑲᕐᕊᑫᑲᕐᕊᑫᑲᕐᕊᑫᑲ **GOLDEN RULE** ᑫᑲᕐᕊᑫᑲᕐᕊᑫᑲᕐᕊᑫᑲᕐᕊᑫᑲ

When you start a new idea in a piece of writing, begin a new *paragraph*.
A paragraph usually has three or more sentences in it.

Play Ball!

There should be four paragraphs in the sports story below. Place the paragraph symbol (¶) wherever you think a new paragraph should begin.

The baseball playoff series between the Hawks and the Ravens started at sundown. A large crowd had gathered to watch the opening matchup between the two undefeated teams. Everyone thought the game would be a close one. In the first three innings, both pitchers were in control. Neither team scored, and no runners went beyond first base. The crowd began to grow restless, and almost everyone visited the hot dog vendor for one of his famous chili dogs. He sold out and had to close his stand early. During the fourth inning, the pace picked up dramatically. The Ravens hit three singles in a row! That cost the Hawks one run. Then the next batter grounded into a double play, as the Ravens' fans hooted and hollered. The rowdy crowd in the bleachers began to dance on top of their seats. Finally, the Hawks came back strong in the bottom of the sixth inning with a two-run homer. The fans were going wild as the two runners tagged home base. One young fan, who was up past his bedtime, had fallen asleep and missed all the excitement.

Can you tell him which team was winning? ___No_____

EXTRA Take out the last story you wrote and look at how you divided it into paragraphs. Did you remember to start a new paragraph for each new idea? Did you develop your ideas so that you have at least three sentences in each paragraph? Then revise your story so that your paragraphs are extra strong.

Name _____ Date _____

ↄↄↄↄↄↄↄↄↄↄↄ **GOLDEN RULE** ↄↄↄↄↄↄↄↄↄↄↄↄↄ

When you start a new idea in a piece of writing, begin a new *paragraph*. Also
start a new paragraph every time a different person speaks. For example,
Maurice tripped and fell. "I can't get up!" he shouted.
His mother ran into the room. "Where are you?" she asked.
"I'm on the floor," he replied.

Homework Blues

**Read the passage below and place the
paragraph symbol (¶) wherever a new
paragraph should begin.**

¶Jason ran down the stairs. "See you later, Mom," he said,
heading out the door. "Freeze!" said his mother, folding her
arms.¶"What's the matter?" asked Jason.¶"Didn't I say you
had to do your homework before you went out?" his
mother reminded him. Jason nodded.¶"It's all done," he
said. His mother arched an eyebrow.¶"Really? I'm impressed,
Jason. It's been only five minutes since you started. It's hard
to believe you could finish everything so quickly.¶"I work fast,
Mom," said Jason. "You know that." His mother laughed.
¶"What I *know* is that you're usually as slow as molasses.¶"I've
changed," said Jason. "Really.¶"I see," said his mother. "So you're
telling me you did all your math problems, started your report outline,
and read a story?" Jason hesitated.¶"Well, I picked out a story to
read," he said slowly. His mother gave him a look.¶"Just march back
upstairs and try again.¶"It's hard being a kid," Jason sighed. His
mother smiled.¶"Sometimes," she said, "it's hard being a mom, too."

ↄↄↄↄↄↄↄↄↄↄↄↄↄↄↄↄↄↄↄↄↄↄↄↄↄↄↄↄↄↄↄↄↄↄↄↄ

EXTRA Write a dialogue between a parent and child in which their roles are
reversed. What kind of "rules" does the child make for the parent,
and how does the parent feel about them?

50 Great Reproducible Writing Workouts Scholastic Professional Books

Name _____ Date _____

Homophones are words that sound alike but have different meanings and are spelled differently.

Bear Necessities

On the lines, write OK for the underlined words that are used correctly. Write a homophone that will fix the incorrect words. You should end up with 9 OKs and 21 corrected homophones.

The <u>bare</u> walked through the forest, looking for dinner.
   1

"The last time I <u>eight</u> was yesterday," he said. "I'm hungry. I
   2

want some <u>meet</u>."
   3

A nearby <u>dear</u> laughed. "You have no <u>close</u> on," she said.
   4   **5**

"Of course not," said the <u>bear</u>. "I'm a <u>bear</u> <u>bare</u>."
   6   **7**   **8**

A <u>flee</u> jumped up on the <u>deer's</u> <u>tale</u>. "I don't wear
   9   **10**   **11**

anything, either," he said.

"Neither do I," said a <u>be</u>, buzzing over a <u>flour</u>.
   12   **13**

The <u>bare</u> looked at the <u>deer</u>. "If I could <u>chews</u> to eat
   14   **15**   **16**

something right now," said the <u>bear</u>, "it <u>would</u> be <u>ewe</u>."
   17   **18**   **19**

"You <u>wood</u> have to catch me first," said the <u>deer</u>. "By the
   20   **21**

time you got <u>hear</u>, I <u>would</u> be gone."
   22   **23**

"<u>Wear</u> would <u>you</u> go?" asked the <u>bear</u>.
   24   **25**   **26**

"Over the <u>rose</u> of bushes and down to the <u>creak</u>."
   27   **28**

The <u>bare</u> sighed. "Then I'll just keep looking and hope I find
   29

something before <u>knight</u> comes."
   30

1. bear
2. ate
3. meat
4. deer
5. clothes
6. OK
7. bare
8. bear
9. flea
10. OK
11. tail
12. bee
13. flower
14. bear
15. OK
16. choose
17. OK
18. OK
19. ~~would~~ you
20. would
21. OK
22. here
23. OK
24. where
25. OK
26. OK
27. rows
28. creek
29. bear
30. night

EXTRA Can you think of five more pairs of homophones? Look up the correct spellings if you are unsure.

50 Great Reproducible Writing Workouts Scholastic Professional Books

GOLDEN RULE

Homophones are words that sound alike but have different meanings and are spelled differently.

Trade-Off

On the lines, write OK for the underlined words that are used correctly. Write a homophone that will fix the incorrect words. You should end up with 5 OKs and 25 corrected homophones.

At a sandy <u>beech</u>, a <u>whale</u> and a <u>towed</u> were speaking.
1   2   3

"The ocean's the place <u>four</u> adventure," said the <u>wail</u>.
4   5

"<u>Witch</u> ocean?" asked the <u>toad</u>.
6   7

"Take your pick," said the whale. "The <u>whether</u> is so
8

unpredictable. Sometimes a <u>missed</u> will rise out of nowhere.
9

<u>Won</u> day the fog was <u>sew</u> thick, I couldn't <u>sea</u> my own <u>tale</u>."
10   11   12   13

"We have <u>fowl</u> <u>weather</u> in <u>hour</u> forest, <u>to</u>," said the toad.
14   15   16   17

"The trees grow <u>so</u> <u>hi</u> that <u>hole</u> days pass when the <u>son</u>
18   19   20   21

never shines."

"<u>Whole</u> <u>daze</u>?" the whale repeated <u>allowed</u>. "I <u>wood</u> like
22   23   24   25

to <u>sea</u> that, and I'd like to see <u>sum</u> trees."
26   27

"I'll bring you a <u>bow</u> from a tree tomorrow," said the toad.
28

"I'll bring you the <u>bough</u> of a sunken ship," said the whale.
29

The toad and the whale went their separate <u>weighs</u>,
30

thinking about what it would be like to be the other.

1. beach
2. OK
3. toad
4. for
5. whale
6. which
7. OK
8. weather
9. mist
10. One
11. so
12. see
13. tail
14. fowl
15. OK
16. our
17. too
18. OK
19. high
20. whole
21. sun
22. OK
23. days
24. aloud
25. would
26. see
27. sow
28. bough
29. low
30. ways

EXTRA

As a class or in small groups, generate a list of commonly misspelled words. **Student task:** Write a one-page story using all of the words from the list spelled correctly. You will have to be creative, and maybe a little bit zany, to be able to use all of the words.

Name _____ Date _____

Be careful! It's easy to confuse two words that are spelled similarly.

Picture Perfect?

Circle the underlined word that makes each sentence correct.

After five <u>minuets / minutes</u> of walking around in the art museum, Paul
                    1

was <u>already / all ready</u> bored. He had seen three <u>pictures / pitchers</u> of old
        2   **3**

people, and none of them looked very happy. <u>There / Their</u> faces looked
                                                      4

grim and unfriendly. <u>Except / Accept</u> for the sculpture of two children
                           5

eating <u>desert / dessert</u>, nobody Paul saw was having a good time. He
            6

wasn't having a good time, either. He thought that looking at old paintings

was even worse <u>than / then</u> being in them.
                    7

Hoping to clear his head, he took a deep <u>breath / breathe</u>. Paul would
                                              8

<u>of / have</u> left right <u>then / than</u> if he had not noticed a splash of red out of
  9   **10**

the corner of his eye. The next room was filled with paintings that looked

like someone had just splattered paint all over them.

"I'm going to try that at home," said Paul. "Now *that* looks fun!"

ᖃᓇᖅ ᖃᓇᖅ ᖃᓇᖅ ᖃᓇᖅ

EXTRA Can you think of tricks to remember the difference between the
above pairs of words? For example, *desert* versus *dessert*.
        Remember that *dessert* has an extra *s* because we always want
extra dessert!

Name _____ Date _____

Over the years, people have made up little ditties to help them remember rules of spelling and grammar. One goes like this: "*i* before *e*, except after *c*, or when sounding like *a* as in *neighbor* and *weigh*." Memorizing this rhyme can be helpful, even if it isn't *always* correct.

Spelling Spies

On the lines, write OK for the underlined words that you think are spelled correctly. Write the correct spelling of the incorrect words.

The spy Jane Blond took a deep breath. She had just returned to her enemy's stronghold on a <u>sliegh</u>₁ to <u>retrieve</u>₂ the secret code. Her foe, Doctor Dire, had <u>recieved</u>₃ the code just that morning from a helpful <u>nieghbor</u>₄. He hoped to <u>achieve</u>₅ his malicious goal of controlling the universe. She was not <u>deceived</u>₆ by his promises to rule peacefully.

Jane would go to any length to stop him. She <u>believed</u>₇ that her plans would succeed, but she feared for the future if Doctor Dire <u>riegned</u>₈. Jane could not <u>concieve</u>₉ of a world run by such evil. Still, she knew the doctor <u>perceived</u>₁₀ it could happen. That made him especially dangerous. Jane had to act fast. She had to <u>relieve</u>₁₁ the world of this evil threat, but time was running out.

1. _____

2. _____

3. _____

4. _____

5. _____

6. _____

7. _____

8. _____

9. _____

10. _____

11. _____

ᏨᏫᎾᏓᏯᎾᏕᏨᎳᏫᎾᎳᏫᏕᏫᏕᎳᏨᎳᏫᎾᎳᏫᏕᏫᏕᎳᏨᎳᏫᎾᎳᏫᏕᏫᏕᎳ

EXTRA Look up any of the underlined words if you are unsure of their definitions and write the definitions here. Then use the underlined words in a paragraph about another Jane Blond and Doctor Dire episode.

Name _____ Date _____

⌇⌇⌇⌇⌇⌇⌇⌇⌇⌇⌇ **GOLDEN RULE** ⌇⌇⌇⌇⌇⌇⌇⌇⌇⌇

In the poem "Jabberwocky," Lewis Carroll made up several words by fitting parts of two existing words together. The best-known example is *chortle*—a blend of *chuckle* and *snort* —which is now considered a regular word.

A Good Fit

Can you guess which words were blended together to form the new words?

   Example: smash (from **smack** + **mash**)

1. **twirl**   (from _____ twist _____ + _____ whirl _____)

2. **motel**   (from _____ motor _____ + _____)

3. **smog**   (from _____ smoke _____ + _____)

4. **brunch**   (from _____ + _____)

5. **squiggle** (from _____ + _____)

6. **telethon** (from _____ + _____)

In the spaces below, invent your own blended words.
Show the original words you used to create the new words.
Can you explain what they mean?

_____ (from _____ + _____)

_____ (from _____ + _____)

_____ (from _____ + _____)

_____ (from _____ + _____)

_____ (from _____ + _____)

_____ (from _____ + _____)

_____ (from _____ + _____)

Name _____ Date _____

GOLDEN RULE

Contractions are words that are made from a combination of two larger words. An *apostrophe* (') takes the place of the letters that were dropped when the two words were combined.

For example, the contraction *didn't* is a combination of the words *did not*. The apostrophe shows where the letter *o* was dropped. Note that *will not* becomes *won't*.

Taste Treat

Replace the words in parentheses by creating a contraction and writing it on the line.

When Hansel and Gretel reached the candy cottage,

(they had) _____ been walking for a long time.
                 1

"(I am) _____ hungry," said Hansel. (He had) _____ eaten only
            2   **3**

a crust of bread for breakfast. "And that cottage looks delicious."

"Maybe we (should not) _____," said Gretel. "We might spoil our dinner."
                              4

"If we (do not) _____ eat the cottage," said Hansel, "we (will not)
                      5

_____ have any dinner."
        6

Gretel (had not) _____ thought of that. "I guess (you are)
                        7

_____ right," she admitted.
        8

"Of course I am," said Hansel. "(I will) _____ go first," he added, taking
                                              9

a bite. "Besides, what harm can it do? (We are) _____ all alone here."
                                                        10

Gretel nodded and took a bite for herself.

EXTRA Write ten sentences using ten different contractions. Try to think of some that were not used in the story. Then write one sentence with as many contractions as you can fit into it.

ᘓᘓᘓᘓᘓᘓᘓᘓ GOLDEN RULE ᘓᘓᘓᘓᘓᘓᘓᘓ

A *complete sentence* contains a *subject* and a *verb*. The sentence is about the *subject*, which is a person, place, or thing. The *verb* is the word that tells what the subject is doing.

Good Sports

The sentences below are missing either the subject or the verb. Add words in the blank spaces to turn each phrase into a complete sentence.

1. A soccer ball _____.

2. The star player _____.

3. _____ yelled and screamed.

4. The big game _____.

5. _____ flew over their heads, out of reach.

6. The head coach _____.

7. The fastest girl on the team _____.

8. _____ bounced into his arms.

9. The exhausted goalie _____.

10. _____ placed the corner kick perfectly.

11. A few of the players _____.

12. _____ won the championship six years in a row.

13. The buzzer went off just as _____.

Name _____ Date _____

A *complete sentence* contains a *subject* and a *verb*. The sentence is about the *subject*, which is a person, place, or thing. The *verb* is the word that describes what the subject is doing.

Holiday Shopping

Create a complete sentence using each phrase.

1. my favorite gift

_____

2. at the top of my list

_____

3. an exciting adventure game

_____

4. lost at the mall

_____

5. three copies of the same book

_____

6. for my sister

_____

7. an electric robot

_____

8. the noisy crowd

_____

28

Name _____ Date _____

A **run-on sentence** has at least two complete ideas jammed together. For example, *We were waiting for the movie to begin, it took so long that we finished all of our refreshments.* The correct way to write this is: *We were waiting for the movie to begin. It took so long that we finished all of our refreshments.*

Take Me to Your Leader

Read the passage below. Then copy it over on the lines provided, breaking up the run-on sentences.

People of Earth! We have come from a distant galaxy that is much farther away than you realize, we come in peace, although you might not think so because of all the laser cannons sticking out of our spaceship. These weapons are much more powerful than anything you possess, we do not want to rub this in because it might hurt your feelings. You have finally found a life-form from another planet, but it is superior to your own, that's life, you'd better get used to it.

_____

_____

_____

_____

_____

_____

_____

_____

_____

EXTRA Write five run-on sentences about life in distant galaxies. Then trade papers with a classmate and fix each other's sentences.

Name _____ Date _____

A **run-on sentence** has at least two complete ideas jammed together. For example, *Recess came too soon today I was still hungry after lunch, next time I'll eat more.* The correct way to write this is: *Recess came too soon today. I was still hungry after lunch. Next time I'll eat more.*

Knight Fears

Read the passage below. Then copy it over on the lines provided, breaking up the run-on sentences.

The knight who was about to fight the dragon was feeling a little nervous, fighting a dragon is not easy there was a chance he would get hurt or burned or stepped on. Still, he had to try because he had promised the villagers they were tired of having their houses burned and their flocks stolen. So the knight went up the mountain, secretly hoping the dragon would not be home then he could go back to the village, he would rather find a safe job like feeding pigs or polishing boots, but he knew that was impossible, no one was safe as long as the dragon remained alive.

_____

_____

_____

_____

_____

_____

_____

_____

_____

_____

EXTRA Write five run-on sentences describing what happened to the knight and the dragon. Then switch papers with a partner and fix each other's sentences.

50 Great Reproducible Writing Workouts Scholastic Professional Books

Name _____ Date _____

A **run-on sentence** has at least two complete ideas jammed together. For example, *In our class people don't have girlfriends or boyfriends they just have plain old friends it's better that way.* The correct way to write this is: *In our class people don't have girlfriends or boyfriends. They just have plain old friends. It's better that way.*

Playing Politics

Read the passage below. Then copy it over on the lines provided, breaking up the run-on sentences.

Well, I'm running for the presidency of our class I have a lot of plans to share with you. I know you've heard promises about getting rid of all homework and making recess twice as long, I favor those things as much as anyone, but we can't make recess last all day if we did that, there would be no time for lunch and gym, sometimes they're important too. I realize that a few of you want to work hard in school, and I don't want to stand in your way, however, I don't want to stand too close to you either because maybe you're contagious.

_____

_____

_____

_____

_____

_____

_____

_____

_____

_____

ᕋ ᑯ ᕋ ᑯ ᕋ ᑯ ᕋ ᑯ ᕋ ᑯ ᕋ ᑯ ᕋ ᑯ ᕋ ᑯ ᕋ ᑯ ᕋ ᑯ ᕋ ᑯ ᕋ ᑯ ᕋ ᑯ ᕋ ᑯ ᕋ

EXTRA Write a convincing paragraph about why you should be elected class president. Make sure you don't have any run-on sentences. As an extra challenge, avoid starting sentences with *I.*

Name _____ Date _____

૯౸౽౨౽౨౯౽౨౯౽౨౽౨౽౨౽ **GOLDEN RULE** ౯౸౽౨౯౽౨౽౨౽౨౽౨

A ***run-on sentence*** has at least two complete ideas jammed together. For example, *My family goes camping in the summer, we hike during the day and toast marshmallows at night.* The correct way to write this is: *My family goes camping in the summer. We hike during the day and toast marshmallows at night.*

Shipshape

Read the passage below. Then copy it over on the lines provided, breaking up the run-on sentences.

   From the moment Denise boarded the ship, she knew she was in for a long day she thought it could possibly be the longest day of her life. In the protected harbor, the lapping waves made her stomach do somersaults she could only imagine how she would feel once the waves got bigger, as the rocking got worse, she turned several shades of green. Everyone else was completely unaware of what would happen if Denise tried to eat lunch, even though they were serving her favorite seafood dish of squid, eel, and snails, she knew that she would be better off not eating a thing.

_____

_____

_____

_____

_____

_____

_____

_____

_____

50 Great Reproducible Writing Workouts Scholastic Professional Books

Name _____ Date _____

Sometimes it's better to combine two related ideas into one sentence to avoid repeating words.

Adding Things Up

Combine each of the pairs of sentences below into one longer sentence that does not repeat words or phrases.

1 sentence
+ 1 sentence
1 sentence

1. My aunt is in the picture. My uncle is in the picture.

_____

2. Trapeze artists are in the circus. Clowns are in the circus.

_____

3. Jupiter goes around the sun. Saturn goes around the sun.

_____

4. Michael is in my class. Jennifer is in my class.

_____

5. The flowers need rain. The trees need rain.

_____

6. London is in Europe. Paris is in Europe.

_____

7. Cucumbers are in the salad. Tomatoes are in the salad.

_____

8. Snow was part of the storm. Wind was part of the storm.

_____

EXTRA Write your own choppy sentences and then combine them.

9. _____   _____

_____

10. _____   _____

_____

Name _____ Date _____

Sometimes it's better to combine two related ideas into one sentence to avoid repeating certain words.

Collision Course

Combine each of the pairs of sentences below into one longer sentence that does not repeat words or phrases.

1. The comet is heading for Earth. The comet will hit tomorrow.

   _____

2. I added flour to the recipe. I added sugar to the recipe.

   _____

3. The racing car hit the wall. The racing car rolled over.

   _____

4. The diver dove into the water. The diver made a big splash.

   _____

5. The wrecking ball swung toward the building. The wrecking ball broke the window.

   _____

6. The hammer hit the nail. The hammer smashed my finger.

   _____

7. The pin was sharp. The pin popped the balloon.

   _____

8. The avalanche roared down the hill. The avalanche destroyed the trees.

   _____

EXTRA Write your own choppy sentences and then combine them.

9. _____   _____

   _____   _____

10. _____   _____

   _____

GOLDEN RULE

To keep your writing from becoming boring, experiment with different sentence structures. Don't begin every sentence with the subject.

We always sit at the round table during lunch.
During lunch, we always sit at the round table.

A piece of pizza suddenly flew across the cafeteria.
Suddenly, a piece of pizza flew across the cafeteria.

(The commas after brief introductory words or phrases are optional.)

Just the Facts

Rewrite each sentence so that it does not begin with the subject.

1. I fell fast asleep during the movie.

_____

2. My brother Larry was born in 1987.

_____

3. The students completed the lab in science class.

_____

4. The movie was over at last.

_____

5. We luckily found our lost cat.

_____

6. The family took a walk after dinner.

_____

7. Lisa will visit her grandfather tomorrow.

_____

8. We will undoubtedly be late for the party.

_____

GOLDEN RULE

A **noun** is a word that identifies a person, place, or thing. It is easy to recognize *people* and *places*, but *things* are more difficult to find. *Things* include everything from *ideas* to *electricity* to *seasickness*. In the sentence "That road is the way out of town," *road* and *town* are clearly nouns, but so is *way*. (Note that pronouns, such as *he, her,* and *they,* also name people, places, and things, but nouns name them more specifically.)

Traffic Jam

Circle all 40 nouns.

The parade started out well. A band played music as the elephants led the way down Main Street. All the performers were there, including the jugglers, clowns, lion tamers, and acrobats.

The problems began when the monkeys escaped from their cages and climbed into the trees. They threw acorns and leaves at the lions and tigers, who roared back at them. The roaring scared the elephants. They turned into an alley that wasn't really wide enough for them to fit through. Even though the horses pulling the wagons knew better than to follow the elephants, they still galloped ahead. The wind knocked loose a huge bunch of balloons, which filled the sky and frightened the monkeys back into their cages.

The only animals who stayed calm were the giraffes. They saw the mess that was developing, and they wisely stood still until things settled down. They watched as the lion tamers shrieked, and they wondered when they would let the giraffes run the show. They were the only creatures that could remain calm in a crisis.

EXTRA Make three columns and label them *People, Places,* and *Things.* List ten nouns in each category and then write a story using all of them.

50 Great Reproducible Writing Workouts Scholastic Professional Books

GOLDEN RULE

A *verb* is a word that describes an action. *Jump, run, talk,* and *play* are all verbs, but so are *think* and *love*. Even just existing or being present is an action. In the sentence "Julia usually skis and skates, but today she is tired," *skis, skates,* and *is* are all verbs.

Shaky Ground

Circle the 26 verbs.

The earthquake hit just before dawn. It came without warning and caught everyone by surprise. Everyone felt the effects immediately. Houses shook, windows rattled, lampposts wobbled, and several telephone poles fell over. Dogs barked, cats screeched, and a few babies screamed at the top of their lungs.

The damage was everywhere. Cracks spread through the streets like spiders' webs. A billboard fell and crushed a parked car. Two trees dropped into giant holes, and only their tops stuck out. In the park, several pipes burst in the fountain, and water poured over the broken benches.

The quake lasted less than a minute, but it seemed like a lot longer to everyone in the middle of it. After the siren sounded "All Clear!," everyone went outside out of curiosity. As they walked around, they saw the incredible damage. Luckily, there were no serious injuries.

EXTRA

In what area are you an expert? Making a peanut butter and jelly sandwich? Scoring a soccer goal? Write a detailed set of directions describing how to do the activity. Make sure that all of your verbs are strong action verbs like the ones in the story.

Name _____ Date _____

GOLDEN RULE

Use *verb tense* to place your writing in the past, present, or future.

Just in Time

The underlined verbs are in the wrong tense.
Write them correctly on the lines.

Alison and Jack have just returned from a journey through time.

"Wow!" said Alison. "We take such an amazing trip."
                          1

Jack agrees. "The dinosaurs sure looked different in real life.
       2

The flying pterodactyls filled the sky."

Alison nods. "I knew dinosaurs were big, but I do not know
        3   4

they are that big. And who would have thought they have so
      5   6

many different colors? The books show them only in brown or

green or gray."

"Yeah," says Jack. "The red styracosaurus catch my attention."
          7   8

Alison laughed. "And they play well together. That one
                              9

tyrannosaurus wanted to play with you."

Jack shudders at the memory. "He wanted to have me for
        10

lunch. His teeth look even bigger up close."
               11

"I am glad we get back here safely," said Alison. "So what
                12

do we did now?"
       13

"Let's had lunch ourselves," said Jack. "I'm as hungry as
        14

any dinosaur."

Entering the Past Tense

1. _____

2. _____

3. _____

4. _____

5. _____

6. _____

7. _____

8. _____

9. _____

10. _____

11. _____

12. _____

13. _____

14. _____

EXTRA Write a short paragraph about dinosaurs in the past tense. Then change the verbs to the present tense so it sounds like dinosaurs are alive today. Finally, change the verbs to the future tense so it sounds like there will be dinosaurs tomorrow! For example: *Some dinosaurs were huge. Some dinosaurs are huge. Some dinosaurs will be huge.*

50 Great Reproducible Writing Workouts Scholastic Professional Books

Name _____ Date _____

Rescue Mission

The underlined verbs do not agree with their subjects. Write the correct verbs on the lines.

The princess sat on the dungeon floor. She turned a spoon

in the keyhole of the door, trying to unlock it.

"What <u>is</u> I going to do? This <u>are</u> a horrible situation!" she cried.
      1   **2**

Suddenly, a stone moved in the wall, and three elves popped out.

"We <u>is</u> here to rescue you!" they shouted. "<u>Isn't</u> you happy
     3   **4**

to see us?"   1. _____

The princess had no time to answer before a grate fell down   2. _____

from the ceiling. A prince jumped down to the floor.   3. _____

"I <u>has</u> come to rescue you," he explained. "You <u>looks</u> awful!"   4. _____
    5   **6**

"We <u>was</u> here first," said one elf. "You <u>needs</u> to leave, Mr. Prince."   5. _____
     7   **8**

A stone moved in the floor. Two soldiers climbed out.   6. _____

"We <u>wants</u> to save you, Princess!" they announced.   7. _____
     9

"Too late," said the prince. "She <u>need</u> me, and only me."   8. _____
                                   10

"No, us!" said the elves. "She <u>are</u> depending on us!"   9. _____
                               11

The princess threw up her hands in disgust. "I <u>is</u> going to   10. _____
                                                12

rescue myself, thank you," she said. And opening the dungeon   11. _____

door, she walked out and slammed it shut behind her.   12. _____

ꙮꙮꙮ

EXTRA Write sentences with these subjects: *I; Sammy; You; We; Ma and Pa.* Now change the subjects in the same sentences and check if you also need to adjust your verbs. New subjects: *Brenda and Mike; I; Lenny; You; We.*

Name _____ Date _____

You can use *conjunctions* to connect two different ideas in a sentence.
These are some common conjunctions:

and   but   if   while   because   so   since   unless   or

The Small Print

In the passage below, fill in the blanks with an
appropriate conjunction. Sometimes more than
one conjunction will work in a sentence.
You may also use them more than once.

Congratulations! You are the proud owner of

the Murgatroyd 2000, the latest in personal

computers _____ the best deal in town. We applaud you
                    1

_____ you chose the finest product available. Before you begin
       2

using it, we suggest you follow a few simple instructions _____
                                                          3

that you don't break it by mistake. The directions are very accurate

_____ they are also difficult to understand, _____
     4   **5**

you are a computer expert. You might want to blame us

_____ anything goes wrong, _____ you should
     6   **7**

really blame yourself for not reading this more closely. _____
                                                          8

your computer crashes _____ you're in the middle of
                           9

something, call our hot line _____ write us a letter describing
                                10

the problem. We might not be able to help you, _____ at least
                                                  11

you'll have a good excuse for why your homework isn't done.

ᒍᕼᒍᕕᕗᒍᕕᒎᒍᕼᒍᕼᒎᒍᕼᕗᕼᒎᕼᒎᕼᕼᒍᕼᒎᕼᕗᒎᕼᒎᕼᒎᕼᕼᒍᕼ

EXTRA Write sentences using each of the conjunctions in the box at the top
of the page.

Name _____ Date _____

ᕽᓄᕮᒃ ᐁᓄᕽ GOLDEN RULE ᒃᕮᓄᓇᕽᓄᓇᕮᓄ

You can use *conjunctions* to connect two different ideas in a sentence.
These are some common conjunctions:

and   but   if   because   so   since   either   or

The Bubble Gum Game

In the game instructions below, fill in the blanks with an appropriate conjunction. Sometimes more than one conjunction will work in a sentence. You may also use them more than once.

I made up a game to play with my friends _____ we were all
                                                    1

tired of playing the same old games. I called it "the bubble gum game"

_____ that my friends would want to play it, _____
        2   3

you can also use other kinds of candy, too. It is good to play year-round

_____ you can play it _____ inside _____
        4   5   6

outside. My mom says it makes you exercise your body _____ your
                                                                7

brain. My friends say they don't like the game anymore, _____
                                                                    8

they still want to play it every day. I told them that they do not have to play it

_____ they do not want to, _____ this is a free
        9   10

country. They said that there is nothing better to do, _____ we still
                                                                11

play the bubble gum game. You can come over to learn how to play it,

_____ you can make up your own game.
        12

ᕽᓄᕮᒃ ᐁᓄᕽᓄᕮᒃᐁᓄᕽᓄᕮᓄᕮᒃᐁᓄᕽᓄᕮᒃᐁᓄᕽᓄᕮᓄᕮᒃᐁ

EXTRA Make up your own game and write instructions for it. Try to use all
of the conjunctions in the box at the top of the page.

Name _____ Date _____

> ***Pronouns*** are words that take the place of nouns. For example, if you write
> "Rip Van Winkle was tired, so he yawned," *he* is a pronoun that substitutes
> for *Rip Van Winkle*. Common pronouns:
>
> > **he   she   they   we   her   him   you   it   our   them   I   us   who**

Play Time

In the passage below, fill in the blanks with
an appropriate pronoun. Some pronouns
may be used more than once.

Thank you for coming to audition for

_____ new play, *Middle Ages Madness*.
       1

The cast features many good roles for _____ to consider.
                                              2

Prepostero is the male lead. _____ is a court jester in the service of
                                    3

Queen Straitlace, who thinks _____ is very wise. _____ is a
                                  4   5

very strict ruler, and _____ twin daughters Griselda and Penelope
                             6

are even stricter. _____ often fight over which of _____ will
                          7   8

be queen after their mother dies. The Duke of Misery doesn't care which

daughter becomes queen as long as _____ can marry _____.
                                         9   10

As _____ in the audience might expect, surprising things happen
        11

to the duke. The plot builds to an exciting climax, but at this moment we

can reveal _____ only to the chosen cast members. We hope you
                12

can understand _____ position. So sign up, and good luck!
                      13

EXTRA   Describe a scene from this play. Refer to Queen Straitlace, the Duke
of Misery, and the other characters by their names. Then replace
their names with pronouns.

Name _____ Date _____

Family Reunion

In the passage below, fill in the blanks with an appropriate pronoun. Some pronouns may be used more than once.

Uncle ~~Fred~~
him   Aunt ~~Bet~~
me

The Getalongs were on their way to a family reunion.

"_____ will be there?" asked Jenny.
         1

"All of _____," said her father. "_____ is a special occasion."
         2   3

"A reunion doesn't feel special," said Jenny's brother, Ben. "Somebody's

going to pinch my cheeks. And somebody else is going to tell _____
                                                              4

how big I've grown." _____ shuddered. "I mean, of course I've
                     5

grown. What else was _____ supposed to do?"
                     6

"Never mind," said their mother. "I expect _____ to behave
                                            7

yourself. Your aunts and uncles haven't seen _____ for a while.
                                              8

_____ have a right to cluck over _____ a little."
9   10

"Maybe," said Jenny. "But when _____ grow up, I'm going to
                               11

be different."

"_____ are different already," said Ben. Then _____ ducked
12   13

for cover.

∽ᴖᴖᴖᴖᴖᴖᴖᴖᴖᴖᴖᴖᴖᴖᴖᴖᴖᴖᴖᴖᴖᴖᴖᴖᴖᴖᴖᴖᴖᴖᴖᴖᴖ

EXTRA Describe a real or imaginary family reunion using lots of names. Then replace all of the names with pronouns.

Name _____ Date _____

ᎶᏊᎶᏒᏊᎧᏚᎶᏊᎧᏋᎶᏚᏐᎶᏚᏐ GOLDEN RULE ᏒᏊᎧᏊᎶᏊᎧᎶᏊᎧᏐᏊᎧᏊᎶᏊᎧ

Just as an adjective describes a noun, an **adverb** is a word that describes a verb. Adverbs answer four questions about verbs:

- **How?** She ran *quickly*.
- **Where?** He ran *there*.
- **When?** I ran *yesterday*.
- **How much?** They run *often*.

School Rules

Read the following passage and then choose adverbs to make it more descriptive and interesting. You can use adverbs from the list in the box, or you can think of your own.

There are several tricks to doing well in Mr. Stubbs's class. First you must _____ remember to arrive _____ every day. When you walk in the door, smile _____. Otherwise he will _____ ask you what is wrong.

During class, you must take notes _____. If you don't, Mr. Stubbs will ask you very _____ if you already know everything. Answer him _____ and _____ tell him that you like his tie.

When Mr. Stubbs is teaching, you must _____ yawn. He also does not like it if you cough _____, but if you cough _____ he might not care. Whatever you do, don't blow your nose _____! He _____ hates that.

Mr. Stubbs uses short sentences that make him sound bossy sometimes. He'll say, "Come _____!" or "Go _____!" or "Do this _____!" You might think he is in a bad mood, but he _____ does not want to waste any time. You will _____ learn a lot in his class.

neatly
quickly
quietly
soon
early
always
usually
not
now
late
often
constantly
loudly
definitely
politely
frequently
fiercely
here
really
casually
never
gently
there
nicely
brightly

ᎶᏊᎶᏒᏊᎧᏚᎶᏊᎧᏋᎶᏚᏐᎶᏚᏐᏟᎶᎶᏊᎧᎶᏊᎧᎶᏊᎧᏊᎶᏊᎧᏊᎶᏊᎧᏊᎶᏊᎧᏊᎶᏊᎧ

EXTRA Write a paragraph describing something you do. Use as many adverbs as you can.

50 Great Reproducible Writing Workouts Scholastic Professional Books

Name _____ Date _____

GOLDEN RULE
Sometimes describing a character with one adjective isn't enough. Remember,
it's the **Big Bad** Wolf who wants those three little pigs.

Animal Traits

Add two adjectives in front of
the following animals to give
each a unique description.

1. _____ _____ **bear**

2. _____ _____ **whale**

3. _____ _____ **unicorn**

4. _____ _____ **eagle**

5. _____ _____ **tyrannosaurus**

6. _____ _____ **dragon**

7. _____ _____ **goat**

8. _____ _____ **puppy**

9. _____ _____ **shark**

10. _____ _____ **moose**

EXTRA Make a list of adjectives that describe yourself. Then make another
list of adjectives that describe the kind of person with whom you like
to be friends.

Name _____   Date _____

GOLDEN RULE

By carefully choosing your words, you can change or sharpen the mood of your writing. For example, a *plant* can become a *beanstalk,* or a *boy* can become an *urchin.* And *walking* down the street can become *sauntering* down the street.

Eating Out

Choose one word from each pair to fill in the blank with the same number.

Last night we went out to eat in a _____ .
1

I noticed that the place seemed _____ ,
2

but I was _____ so I just ordered.
3

I decided to have a _____ . There were
4

_____ forks and knives on the table. I put
5

a _____ napkin on my lap before the meal
6

came. For dessert I had chocolate _____ .
7

It was _____ and tasted great with my tall
8

glass of _____ . Luckily, I didn't spill any on
9

my _____ shirt. When I got home, I had a
10

snack before going to bed.

1. <u>restaurant   diner</u>

2. <u>deserted   quiet</u>

3. <u>hungry   starving</u>

4. <u>hot dog   steak</u>

5. <u>silver   plastic</u>

6. <u>linen   paper</u>

7. <u>pudding   mousse</u>

8. <u>gooey   creamy</u>

9. <u>milk   soda</u>

10. <u>silk   polyester</u>

EXTRA Write about what it's like to eat at your favorite restaurant. Then change certain words to make it somewhere you would never want to eat.
Example: *I always order a juicy steak at Sirloin Palace.*
I always order dry meatloaf at Elmore's Greasy Drive-Thru.

50 Great Reproducible Writing Workouts Scholastic Professional Books

Name _____ Date _____

By carefully choosing your words, you can change or sharpen the mood of your writing. For example, a *rock* can become a *diamond,* or a *creature* can become a *dragon.*

Quick Visit

In the passage below, fill in the blanks by substituting one of the words in the box for each highlighted word. Words that appear more than once, such as *prince,* should have the same substitute each time.

A **prince** _____ 1 _____ dressed in **armor** _____ 2 _____

rode up to the **castle** _____ 3 _____ and knocked on the door.

Nobody answered, so the **prince** _____ 4 _____ went inside.

The walls were piled high with **treasure** _____ 5 _____. The

prince _____ 6 _____ searched through it quickly.

Suddenly he heard a **shout** _____ 7 _____.

"Who's there?" asked the **giant** _____ 8 _____ who owned

the **castle** _____ 9 _____.

The **prince** _____ 10 _____ didn't answer. He grabbed some

jewels _____ 11 _____ and shoved them in his pocket. Then he

ran _____ 12 _____ away and lived **happily** _____ 13 _____

ever after.

walked
trash
peasant
young girl
whisper
quietly
stones
barn
farmer
cottage
rags
hay

EXTRA Write a list of 20 nondescript (general) words. Then change them to more specific and interesting words.

Examples: *vegetable—eggplant   pet—iguana   talking—chatting*

Name _____ Date _____

You can change the mood of a piece of writing by using very specific descriptive words instead of general words. For example, a *feeling* can become a *sudden chill,* or a *car* can turn into a *red convertible.*

This Spooky Old House

Read the following passage and then create substitutes (up to three words) for each of the highlighted words to make the passage feel spooky and mysterious.

I approached the door to the **house** _____
1

with mixed feelings. I wasn't sure anyone was home, although I had

seen a **light** _____ in the upstairs window. As I knocked
2

on the door, I thought I heard a **noise** _____ from inside.
3

No one answered the knock. I heard that **sound** _____
4

again. Maybe I should go inside to see what was happening. When I tried the

door _____, I found it was unlocked.
5

I went inside. In the darkness, I saw **something** _____
6

move across the floor. The door swung shut **loudly** _____
7

behind me, and suddenly I had the feeling I was not alone. Up ahead in the

darkness _____, I thought I could make out a
8

shape _____. I wasn't sure. I was sure, though, that
9

coming inside might have been a **mistake** _____. I turned
10

around to leave, but the door was mysteriously locked!

ᠻᠣᠾᠻᠣᠳᢉᠻᠣᠴᠣᠾᠣᠴᠣᠾᠣᠴᢉᠻᢉᠲᠳᠥᠹᢉᠾᢉᠾᠻᠣᠾᠻᠣᠳᢉᠲᠳᠥᠹᢉᠾᠣᠾ

EXTRA Describe a creepy scene and try to make the reader feel nervous by using descriptive words.

50 Great Reproducible Writing Workouts Scholastic Professional Books

Name _____ Date _____

To make your writing come alive, include descriptions that involve all five
senses.

Sense-itivity

Fill in the spaces with two opposite choices from
the lists below. Note how differently the passage
reads depending on which words you choose.

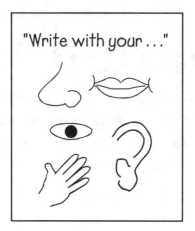

"Write with your . . ."

The other day we went to the beach. It was a

_____|_____ day. Many people were there.
        1

The air smelled _____|_____. As we walked
                        2

along barefoot, the sand felt _____|_____
                                      3

between our toes. When I went swimming, I accidentally

swallowed some water. It tasted _____|_____.
                                        4

After I got out, I was tired, so I lay down for a nap. Every time

I shut my eyes, though, I heard a _____|_____.
                                          5

I didn't sleep at all, but I did get a terrible sunburn.

1 **Sight**	2 **Smell**	3 **Touch**	4 **Taste**	5 **Sound**
bright	fresh	soft	bitter	buzz
sunny	clean	cold	sour	splash
hazy	smoky	sharp	salty	hiss
foggy	musty	smooth	sweet	thump
glowing	fragrant	sticky	spicy	growl

ᘛᑫᖘᑫᕽᑫᕽᖘᑫᖘᖘᑫᕽᖘᑫᖘᖘᑫᕽᘛᑫᖘᖘᑫᖘᑫᕽᖘᑫᖘᖘᑫᖘᑫᕽ

EXTRA Write your own vivid description using all five senses. Try to use
your own experiences to make it seem real.

Name _____ Date _____

You can use **adjectives** (words that describe a person, place, or thing) to give characters a specific personality. For example, *a purring cat* is different from *a hissing cat.*

Second Look

When writing stories, sometimes you start out thinking one way about a character but later change your mind. In the examples below, change the description of each character.

1. a hairy monkey

_____

2. the big bad wolf

_____

3. the shy king

_____

4. a crying baby

_____

5. the cute puppy

_____

6. the polite guest

_____

7. the fierce giant

_____

8. the careful turtle

_____

9. the rusty pail

_____

ᏀᎾᎯᏓᎬᏌᎫᏋᏓᎬᏟᎾᎬᏁᏡᏐᏉᎬᏓᏇᎾᎬᎦᎬᏁᎦᏍᏐᏉᏋᏡᏐᏁᏇᎾᎬᏁᎾᎦᏌᏓᏦᎲᏎᏓᎾᎬᎦᏐ

EXTRA Make a list of ten nouns. Switch papers with a partner and add adjectives to describe the nouns. Then switch back and change the adjectives so that they are very different.

GOLDEN RULE
Unnecessary words make a piece of writing seem boring or confusing.

Running Late

Read the passage below and cross out unnecessary words or sentences.

On the very first day of school, Jennifer was late. She didn't make it to school on time. She was ten years old, but would be eleven on her next birthday. On the way to school, she had been listening to the *Amazon River Rats*, who had sold more than ten million CDs. They are very popular.

Mrs. Wilton, her teacher who taught her math, science, English, and other subjects, was not interested in Jennifer's excuses. She had struggled with her own personal problems that morning after eating her usual daily breakfast of a poached egg on toast. She had gotten stuck in traffic behind several cars: three red cars, two blue cars, and one purple van. One driver, who was driving a purple van, kept honking his horn repeatedly, over and over again.

"If *I* can get here on time, Jennifer," said Mrs. Wilton, checking her ancient watch with the old, worn leather band, "so can *you*." She had worn that watch every day for twenty years, day in and day out. In fact, this was the very same watch she used to look at anxiously and nervously when she was running late to school as a kid in various grades.

EXTRA Write a real or imaginary description about getting to school that is intentionally too wordy. Then switch papers with a partner and eliminate the unnecessary words.

Name _____ Date _____

Aches and Pains

Read the passage below and cross out unnecessary words or phrases.

ON AIR

Are you one of the millions of the many Americans living in the United States in houses or apartments who suffer from painful headaches? Have you wished in vain for some kind of temporary relief from the steady pounding that doesn't stop, but just seems to go on and on? If so, then we have news for you if you just keep reading. For just $19.95 in dollars and cents, we will send you our new headache stopper—PainBane. It is not available in any stores, whether or not they're big or small or sell other things. It is available only through this special TV offer you're listening to right now. Act now, and we'll also send you PainGain, which works in just the opposite way. So don't waste another second or minute. Pick up that phone and dial. Operators are standing by with their shoes and socks on, ready to answer your call.

EXTRA
Write a one-minute commercial for a product. Then imagine that you have to fit the whole commercial into 30 seconds. (Talking faster won't do the trick!) Try to get the same message across in half as many words.

Name _____ Date _____

ᖫᖫᖫᖫᖫᖫᖫᖫᖫᖫᖫᖫ **GOLDEN RULE** ᖫᖫᖫᖫᖫᖫᖫᖫᖫᖫᖫᖫ

When we speak, we often use common sayings (known as *idioms*) to suggest the meaning in a situation instead of describing it directly. In writing, however, idioms often muddle the meaning. Use idioms sparingly to clarify your writing.

Up a Creek

The passage below uses several idioms strung together. On the lines provided, rewrite the passage using ordinary words or descriptions.

We're in hot water now. We would have been free and clear if you had buttoned your lip. But, no, you had to let the cat out of the bag. That's why I gave you a dirty look. I wanted to tell you to go fly a kite or at least jump in a lake. But since you're off your rocker, I'll be satisfied if you just get out of my hair. If we're lucky, we'll still escape by the skin of our teeth. If not, that's the way the cookie crumbles.

_____

_____

_____

_____

_____

_____

_____

_____

_____

ᖫᖫᖫᖫᖫᖫᖫᖫᖫᖫᖫᖫᖫᖫᖫᖫᖫᖫᖫᖫᖫᖫᖫᖫᖫᖫᖫᖫ

EXTRA Think of five idioms and then write what they really mean.

Name _____ Date _____

Welcome Matt

**Writers choose among synonyms for just the right word. Each
word in the box is a synonym for one of the highlighted words
in the passage below. Match each synonym with its partner by
filling the blanks next to the highlighted words.**

stare
determine
everybody
instructor
sack
sort
village
despised
fortunate
permanently

   Matt **hated** _____ moving to a new
1

town _____. It meant going to a new school
2

where **everyone** _____ already knew one
3

another. The worst part was being introduced to his class.

Some of the kids would be friendly, but most of them

would hang back, trying to **decide** _____
4

what **kind** _____ of kid he was. They would
5

look _____ at him and he would stare back
6

until the **teacher** _____ told him to take a seat.
7

   If he were **lucky** _____, Matt would have a
8

better time at lunch. He had a plan for that. A whole **bag**

_____ of chocolate chip cookies might not
9

make him popular **forever** _____, but they
10

would certainly help break the ice.

EXTRA Make a list of ten pairs of synonyms. Working with a partner, read
the first word in each pair and see if your partner can guess the
synonym. Then try to guess your partner's synonyms.

Name _____ Date _____

🝔🝔🝔🝔🝔🝔🝔🝔 GOLDEN RULE 🝔🝔🝔🝔🝔🝔🝔🝔

Antonyms are words with opposite meanings, such as *short* and *tall*, *big* and *small*.

Garage Sale

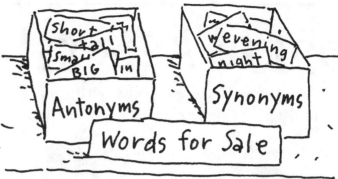

Each word in the box is an antonym for one of the highlighted words in the passage below. Match each antonym with its partner by filling the blanks next to the highlighted words.

Every weekend my **dad** _____ goes to garage sales.
                              1

Sometimes I go with **him** _____. I can't believe what
                               2

people think they can **sell** _____. They spread out their
                                  3

stuff all **over** _____ their yards (or in their garages if it's
                      4

rainy _____).
            5

The stuff all looks like **junk** _____ to me. My
                                     6

dad disagrees. He thinks I don't look closely enough. Those

rusty _____ candlesticks are **valuable** _____,
            7   8

he says. And that chair with the missing leg wobbles only when you

lean to the **left** _____.
                        9

I'm not convinced. I'm still waiting for the **day** _____
                                                        10

when somebody actually puts a price tag on his garage. Now that's a

sale I'd **love** _____ to see.
                     11

hate
treasure
buy
worthless
right
mom
night
under
gleaming
sunny
her

🝔🝔🝔🝔🝔🝔🝔🝔🝔🝔🝔🝔🝔🝔🝔🝔🝔🝔

EXTRA Make a list of ten pairs of antonyms. Working with a partner, read the first word in each pair and see if your partner can guess the antonym. Then try to guess your partner's antonyms.

Name _____ Date _____

ᎶᎤᎶᎶᎠᎠᎾᎢᎬᎶᏈᎬᏋᎶᎬᏁ GOLDEN RULE ᎾᎬᎶᎶᎠᎠᎢᎾᎶᎬᎾᏋᎶᎬᏁ

Try to use specific details in your writing. Words like *thing* or *stuff* don't give enough information for the reader to understand what you're saying.

Some Assembly Required

Replace the underlined words with specific words that will give the directions real meaning.

Before starting, check to make sure you're not missing any

parts. Then gather all of the <u>stuff</u> that you will need to put

1

the <u>thing</u> together. Read these directions at least three times,

2

just in case they are confusing. To begin, find all the

<u>doohickeys</u> and connect them to the <u>thingamabobs</u>. Make

3   4

sure the <u>whatchamacallits</u> are all facing up and that the

5

<u>gizmos</u> can spin freely. Then fasten the <u>gadget</u> to the top so

6   7

that nothing will leak out when you turn it on. After you've

checked that the <u>whoseewhatsits</u> are firmly attached, switch

8

on the <u>doodad</u>. If nothing happens, take all of the pieces

9

apart and start over. (Any leftover pieces should be shoved

into the <u>widget</u> so that nobody will know you left them out.)

10

1. _____

2. _____

3. _____

4. _____

5. _____

6. _____

7. _____

8. _____

9. _____

10. _____

 50 Great Reproducible Writing Workouts Scholastic Professional Books

Answer Key

Capital Crime, page 7

<u>m</u>other goose stood up before the crowd. "Simmer down there, <u>t</u>om <u>t</u>humb. And you, too, <u>b</u>o <u>p</u>eep."

The pigs and sheep continued to mill around.

"As you know," <u>m</u>other goose continued, "someone has stolen the capital letters from our names."

"I knew something was wrong," said <u>c</u>hicken <u>l</u>ittle.

"Stay calm," said <u>p</u>eter <u>p</u>iper.

"That's right," said <u>m</u>other goose. "I'm sure we will get our letters back."

"How long will it take?" asked <u>h</u>umpty <u>d</u>umpty.

"I hope it won't take too long," said <u>m</u>iss <u>m</u>uffet. <u>j</u>ack and <u>j</u>ill nodded.

"Are there any suspects?" asked the Big Bad Wolf, as he put something in his pocket.

"Not yet," said <u>m</u>other goose, clucking. "But I bet you didn't know that I used to be a private investigator. I'll have this solved in no time, and then we'll write a nursery rhyme about it."

Who do you think is the thief? <u>the Big Bad Wolf</u>

Lost in Place, page 8

"You're lost," I told my father.

"I'm not lost," he snapped. "Just a little, um, misplaced."

"Maybe we should ask for directions."

"Don't panic. We can retrace our steps. Let's see…. We came off the highway and passed graham <u>r</u>oad and <u>e</u>lden <u>c</u>ircle. Then we took a right on <u>m</u>ain <u>s</u>treet, a left on <u>m</u>idtown <u>a</u>venue, followed by a quick right on apple <u>t</u>ree <u>l</u>ane until it turned into <u>m</u>acintosh <u>c</u>ircle."

"Uh-oh," I said. "I think we were supposed to go left on apple <u>t</u>ree <u>l</u>ane and then left again on <u>t</u>rotting horse <u>d</u>rive."

My father hesitated. "What if we keep going straight?"

I looked at the map. "It's a dead end."

"All right," he said. "Then we should go back to the intersection of apple <u>t</u>ree <u>l</u>ane and <u>m</u>idtown <u>a</u>venue."

"Maybe we should stop at a gas station to ask for directions."

"No, never!" my dad exclaimed. "I know exactly where I am. And don't worry. I'll get you to the party before it ends."

Capital Capitals, page 9

Brian was pacing back and forth in his room. His mother was standing in the doorway.

"I hate tests on state capitals!" he shouted.

"Of course you do," said his mother. "Now, what's next?"

"<u>o</u>klahoma has the right idea," said Brian. "<u>o</u>klahoma <u>c</u>ity. It's easy. Why can't they all be like that? <u>k</u>ansas has a <u>k</u>ansas <u>c</u>ity, but they wasted it and used <u>t</u>opeka instead."

His mother smiled.

"At least people should make up their minds about the kind of city they want." Brian shook his head. "I mean, look at <u>b</u>oston, <u>m</u>assachusetts, or <u>a</u>tlanta, <u>g</u>eorgia, or <u>d</u>es <u>m</u>oines, <u>i</u>owa. Each is the biggest city in its state. But is that a rule? No. In <u>i</u>llinois, it's <u>s</u>pringfield, not <u>c</u>hicago. In <u>w</u>ashington, it's <u>o</u>lympia, not <u>s</u>eattle. In <u>p</u>ennsylvania, they have two big cities, <u>p</u>hiladelphia and <u>p</u>ittsburgh—and they picked <u>h</u>arrisburg instead."

"You know," said his mother, "you're doing very well."

Brian shrugged. "Maybe," he admitted. "If I get an A on my test, can we go to <u>h</u>onolulu? It's the state capital of <u>h</u>awaii!"

Travel Journal, page 10

What a trip this has been so far! First, we flew to <u>m</u>iami, after stopping off in <u>n</u>ew <u>y</u>ork to change planes. The ride was a little bumpy, but not as bad as the one we took last year to <u>c</u>hicago. I still remember how my lunch went flying off my tray.

Our cruise left <u>m</u>iami at sunset. As we waved good-bye to the <u>u</u>nited <u>s</u>tates, we looked ahead to our trip through the <u>c</u>aribbean. Our schedule called for visits to many islands as well as <u>m</u>exico and <u>v</u>enezuela. Luckily the trip was not as hectic as the one we took two years ago to <u>s</u>outh <u>a</u>merica and <u>e</u>urope. We went to <u>s</u>pain, <u>f</u>rance, and <u>i</u>taly all in one week. I've never eaten so much delicious food!

Two days later we stopped in <u>p</u>uerto <u>r</u>ico. From there we sailed on to <u>b</u>arbados and <u>j</u>amaica. The seas were rough on the first night. Almost everyone was seasick after the all-you-could-eat buffet. Luckily, I was so tired from playing shuffleboard all day that I slept right through the stormy weather. Now the sky is clear and the sea is smooth as glass as we make our way back to the <u>u</u>nited <u>s</u>tates.

Title Search, page 11

1. The Frog Croaks at Midnight
2. Missing Notes of the Rubber Band
3. Stealing Base 5
4. The Vanishing Varnish
5. Eyes of the Potato
6. The Rise and Fall of Argyle Socks
7. Birds of a Feather in the Heather
8. Out of Air at the Balloon Factory

CD-ROAM, page 12

"<u>w</u>hat's that?" <u>i</u> asked at the computer store.

"<u>a</u> miracle," said the salesman. <u>he</u> held up a set of shiny <u>cd</u>-<u>rom</u>s. "<u>i</u> have here the complete phone books of every country in the world."

"<u>y</u>ou're kidding! <u>w</u>hat's it called?"

"*<u>t</u>he <u>o</u>nly <u>p</u>hone <u>b</u>ook <u>y</u>ou'll <u>e</u>ver <u>n</u>eed*. <u>e</u>very continent—<u>a</u>sia, <u>a</u>frica, <u>n</u>orth <u>a</u>merica, <u>s</u>outh <u>a</u>merica, <u>e</u>urope, and <u>a</u>ustralia—is included."

"<u>w</u>hat about <u>a</u>ntarctica?"

"<u>s</u>orry. <u>t</u>here are no phone books there, but we've got everything from <u>t</u>imbuktu to <u>k</u>alamazoo, from <u>k</u>uala <u>l</u>umpur to the house next door. <u>w</u>hat do you think?"

"<u>t</u>hat really is amazing. <u>i</u>'m surprised it's all in <u>e</u>nglish, though."

<u>t</u>he salesman hesitated. "<u>d</u>id <u>i</u> say that? <u>t</u>here's certainly a lot in <u>e</u>nglish, but there are other languages, too. <u>i</u> don't suppose you speak <u>s</u>wahili, <u>f</u>rench, or <u>t</u>hai?"

"<u>s</u>orry," <u>i</u> said. "<u>i</u> don't know all those languages yet. <u>w</u>hen <u>i</u> learn them, <u>i</u>'ll be back."

No Secrets, page 13

"Okay, we're all here," said Amanda. "Now what are we supposed to talk about?"

She looked around the clubhouse.

Mariel just shook her head.

Peter rubbed his chin.

"Come on," said Mariel. "Somebody must have an idea."

"I used up all my ideas yesterday," said Scott.

"On what?" asked Mariel.

Scott looked embarrassed. "I don't remember, but they're gone now. That's for sure."

Peter smiled. "I know why this is so hard," he said. "It's because this is a secret meeting."

"So?" said Mariel.

"Well," Peter went on, "whatever happens at a secret meeting is a secret, so that's why we don't know."

Mariel rolled her eyes. "But we're the ones having the meeting! If we don't know the reason, who will?"

Peter shrugged. "That's why it's such a good secret," he explained.

The Big Mess, page 14

"Look at this room!" my father gasped. "It's a mess."

I looked around. The room seemed fine to me.

"I know where everything is," I told him.

My dad folded his arms. "How can you say that? Your desk is covered with papers. . . ."

"Important papers," I insisted.

"How can you find anything there?"

"I have my own system. It's, um, complicated."

Dad was not impressed. "And the floor is covered with dirty laundry!"

"I was planning to sort it."

He laughed. "In what century? And what about your bed? It's a wonder you don't hurt yourself on all the toys."

"I think you're overreacting."

He shook his head. "I don't. I would say a bomb hit this place, except then I'd see a crater or something. Now I want you to clean this all this up. Okay?"

I nodded but didn't reply. Sometimes parents can be tough.

Touring the Zoo, page 15

Welcome to the City Zoo! We ask that you listen closely☐ to the following description☐ which we will try to keep brief. To your left☐ is our Primate Habitat☐ home of our monkeys☐ chimpanzees☐ orangutans☐ and gorillas. Straight ahead is the Reptile House. This is where our snakes☐ alligators☐ and various lizards wriggle and squirm about. Beyond the Reptile House☐ is our savannah and jungle landscape. Here you will find lions☐ tigers☐ antelopes☐ and elephants. We keep them separated so that everyone stays happy. We also invite you to visit our bird sanctuary. Our curators☐ have gathered birds from all over the world. We have everything from kakapos☐ to egrets. If you have any questions☐ please don't hesitate to ask. Enjoy your visit and remember that while you watch the animals☐ the animals☐ are also watching you!

Stranded, page 16

When the spaceship crash-landed on the planet☐ its captain knew his crew was in trouble☐ This sector was outside the usual travel lanes☐ and they were there only because the gravitational pull of a black hole had pulled them off course☐

"Not too much damage to the ship☐ Captain☐" reported the chief engineer☐ "Life support is holding☐ and the hull suffered only minor cuts and bruises☐"

The captain looked surprised☐ "Well☐ let's prepare to leave☐"

"I was afraid you'd say that☐" said the chief engineer☐ "Unfortunately☐ the engines are off-line☐ We could be here for a long time if no one answers our distress call☐"

"In that case☐" said the captain☐ "I'll have a chance to catch up on my reading☐ Carry on☐"

The captain opened his favorite science fiction book, *Lost in Space for Eternity*☐ The chief engineer wondered how he could read a book like that at a time like this.

The Mad Scientist, page 17
Some answers may vary.

The mad scientist was standing in his secret laboratory. "Soon," he said, "all of my hard work will finally pay off!"

A voice laughed from across the room.

The mad scientist spun around and stared at his assistant, Igor. "Did you say something?"

"Who? Me?" said Igor. "I don't think so."

The mad scientist frowned. "I was sure I heard something."

Igor shrugged. "Are you sure?"

"I said that my work was nearing an end. I am almost ready to conquer the world!"

"Ha, ha!"

The mad scientist wagged a finger at Igor. "This time I saw you laughing!"

"So?" Igor folded his arms. "Let's just say I've heard those words before."

"Well, this time I mean it! And if you don't act more supportive, you can start looking for another job. Do you think there are many mad scientists out there looking for assistants? Think again!"

Three-Ring Circus, page 18
Some answers may vary.

"Ladies and gentlemen," said the ringmaster, "welcome to our circus! Are you glad to be here?"

"Yessss!" shouted the crowd.

The ringmaster smiled broadly. "We have brought together stupendous acts from all over the world!"

The crowd cheered.

"We have Shorty the Lion Tamer," the ringmaster continued. "Is he really as brave as you think? You will be amazed!"

"Oooooh!" said the crowd.

"We also have daring men and women who defy gravity on the flying trapeze! But will they be able to defy it tonight? Who knows? And last, we have the Great Blunderbuss, who will be shot out of a cannon! Do you want to see him land on the moon?"

"Hooray!" cheered the crowd.

The ringmaster smiled. "Get ready for the most exciting show on earth!"

Play Ball!, page 19
¶The baseball playoff series between the Hawks and the Ravens started at sundown. A large crowd had gathered to watch the opening matchup between the two undefeated teams. Everyone thought the game would be a close one. ¶In the first three innings, both pitchers were in control. Neither team scored, and no runners went beyond first base. The crowd began to grow restless, and almost everyone visited the hot dog vendor for one of his famous chili dogs. He sold out and had to close his stand early. ¶During the fourth inning, the pace picked up dramatically. The Ravens hit three singles in a row! That cost the Hawks one run. Then the next batter grounded into a double play, as the Ravens' fans hooted and hollered. The rowdy crowd in the bleachers began to dance on top of their seats. ¶Finally, the Hawks came back strong in the bottom of the sixth inning with a two-run homer. The fans were going wild as the two runners tagged home base. One young fan, who was up past his bedtime, had fallen asleep and missed all the excitement.

The winning team: Hawks 2–1

Homework Blues, page 20
¶Jason ran down the stairs. "See you later, Mom," he said, heading out the door. ¶"Freeze!" said his mother, folding her arms. ¶"What's the matter?" asked Jason. ¶"Didn't I say you had to do your homework before you went out?" his mother reminded him. ¶Jason nodded. "It's all done," he said. ¶His mother arched an eyebrow. "Really? I'm impressed, Jason. It's been only five minutes since you started. It's hard to believe you could finish everything so quickly." ¶"I work fast, Mom," said Jason. "You know that." ¶His mother laughed. "What I *know* is that you're usually as slow as molasses." ¶"I've changed," said Jason. "Really." ¶"I see," said his mother. "So you're telling me you did all your math problems, started your report outline, and read a story?" ¶Jason hesitated. "Well, I picked out a story to read," he said slowly. ¶His mother gave him a look. "Just march back upstairs and try again." ¶"It's hard being a kid," Jason sighed. ¶His mother smiled. "Sometimes," she said, "it's hard being a mom, too."

Bear Necessities, page 21
1. bear
2. ate
3. meat
4. deer
5. clothes
6. OK
7. bare
8. bear
9. flea
10. OK
11. tail
12. bee
13. flower
14. bear
15. OK
16. choose
17. OK
18. OK
19. you
20. would

21. OK
22. here
23. OK
24. Where
25. OK
26. OK
27. rows
28. creek
29. bear
30. night

Trade-Off, page 22
1. beach
2. OK
3. toad
4. for
5. whale
6. Which
7. OK
8. weather
9. mist
10. One
11. so
12. see
13. tail
14. foul
15. OK
16. our
17. too
18. OK
19. high
20. whole
21. sun
22. OK
23. days
24. aloud
25. would
26. see
27. some
28. bough
29. bow
30. ways

Picture Perfect, page 23
1. minutes
2. already
3. pictures
4. Their
5. Except
6. dessert
7. than
8. breath
9. have
10. then

Spelling Spies, page 24
1. sleigh
2. OK
3. received
4. neighbor
5. OK
6. OK
7. OK
8. reigned
9. conceive
10. OK
11. OK

A Good Fit, page 25
2. motor + hotel
3. smoke + fog
4. breakfast + lunch
5. squirm + wiggle (or wriggle)
6. television + marathon

Answers will vary. These are possibilities.

tout   (from tall + stout)
shin   (from short + thin)
sneal   (from snack + meal)
swacket (from sweater + jacket)
frister   (from friend + sister)
frother   (from friend + brother)

Taste Treat, page 26
1. they'd
2. I'm
3. He'd
4. shouldn't
5. don't
6. won't
7. hadn't
8. you're
9. I'll
10. We're

Good Sports, page 27
Answers will vary. These are possibilities.

1. A soccer ball landed on the field.
2. The star player dribbled the ball down the field.
3. All of the fans yelled and screamed.
4. The big game was exciting.
5. The ball flew over their heads, out of reach.
6. The head coach called a time-out.
7. The fastest girl on the team scored a goal.
8. Suddenly, the ball bounced into his arms.
9. The exhausted goalie needed a rest.
10. One of the players placed the corner kick perfectly.
11. A few of the players did not think their team would win.
12. My favorite team won the championship six years in a row.

13. The buzzer went off just as <u>the winning goal was scored</u>.

Holiday Shopping, page 28

Answers will vary. These are possibilities.

1. Chocolate is *my favorite gift.*
2. A toy truck is *at the top of my list.*
3. I played *an exciting adventure game.*
4. Billy was *lost at the mall* for hours.
5. She received *three copies of the same book.*
6. I bought a tennis racket *for my sister.*
7. Did you find *an electric robot* at the toy store?
8. *The noisy crowd* at the mall gave me a headache.

Take Me to Your Leader, page 29

Some answers may vary.

People of Earth! We have come from a distant galaxy that is much farther away than you realize. We come in peace, although you might not think so because of all the laser cannons sticking out of our spaceship. These weapons are much more powerful than anything you possess. We do not want to rub this in because it might hurt your feelings. You have finally found a life form from another planet, but it is superior to your own. That's life. You'd better get used to it.

Knight Fears, page 30

Some answers may vary.

The knight who was about to fight the dragon was feeling a little nervous. Fighting a dragon is not easy. There was a chance he would get hurt or burned or stepped on. Still, he had to try because he had promised the villagers. They were tired of having their houses burned and their flocks stolen. So the knight went up the mountain, secretly hoping the dragon would not be home. Then he could go back to the village. He would rather find a safe job like feeding pigs or polishing boots, but he knew that was impossible. No one was safe as long as the dragon remained alive.

Playing Politics, page 31

Some answers may vary.

Well, I'm running for the presidency of our class. I have a lot of plans to share with you. I know you've heard promises about getting rid of all homework and making recess twice as long. I favor those things as much as anyone, but we can't make recess last all day. If we did that, there would be no time for lunch and gym. Sometimes they're important too. I realize that a few of you want to work hard in school, and I don't want to stand in your way. However, I don't want to stand too close to you either because maybe you're contagious.

Shipshape, page 32

Some answers may vary.

From the moment Denise boarded the ship, she knew she was in for a long day. She thought it could possibly be the longest day of her life. In the protected harbor, the lapping waves made her stomach do somersaults. She could only imagine how she would feel once the waves got bigger. As the rocking got worse, she turned several shades of green. Everyone else was completely unaware of what would happen if Denise tried to eat lunch. Even though they were serving her favorite seafood dish of squid, eel, and snails, she knew that she would be better off not eating a thing.

Adding Things Up, page 33

1. My aunt and uncle are in the picture.
2. Trapeze artists and clowns are in the circus.
3. Jupiter and Saturn go around the sun.
4. Michael and Jennifer are in my class.
5. The flowers and trees need rain.
6. London and Paris are in Europe.
7. Cucumbers and tomatoes are in the salad.
8. Snow and wind were parts of the storm.

Collision Course, page 34

1. The comet is heading for Earth and will hit tomorrow.
2. I added flour and sugar to the recipe.
3. The racing car hit the wall and rolled over.
4. The diver dove into the water and made a big splash.
5. The wrecking ball swung toward the building and broke the window.
6. The hammer hit the nail and smashed my finger.
7. The pin was sharp and popped the balloon.
8. The avalanche roared down the hill and destroyed the trees.

Just the Facts, page 35

1. During the movie, I fell fast asleep.
2. In 1987, my brother Larry was born.
3. In science class, the students completed the lab.
4. At last, the movie was over.
5. Luckily, we found our lost cat.
6. After dinner the family took a walk.
7. Tomorrow Lisa will visit her grandfather.
8. Undoubtedly, we will be late for the party.

Traffic Jam, page 36

The <u>parade</u> started out well. A <u>band</u> played <u>music</u> as the <u>elephants</u> led the <u>way</u> down <u>Main Street</u>. All the <u>performers</u> were there, including the <u>jugglers</u>, <u>clowns</u>, <u>lion tamers</u>, and <u>acrobats</u>.

The <u>problems</u> began when the <u>monkeys</u> escaped from their <u>cages</u> and climbed into the trees. They threw <u>acorns</u> and <u>leaves</u> at the <u>lions</u> and <u>tigers</u>, who roared back at them. The <u>roaring</u> scared the <u>elephants</u>. They turned into an <u>alley</u> that wasn't really wide enough for them to fit through. Even though the <u>horses</u> pulling the <u>wagons</u> knew better than to follow the <u>elephants</u>, they still galloped ahead. The <u>wind</u> knocked loose a huge <u>bunch</u> of <u>balloons</u>, which filled the <u>sky</u> and frightened the <u>monkeys</u> back into their <u>cages</u>.

The only <u>animals</u> who stayed calm were the <u>giraffes</u>. They saw the <u>mess</u> that was developing, and they wisely stood still until <u>things</u> settled down. They watched as the <u>lion tamers</u> shrieked, and they wondered when would they let the <u>giraffes</u> run the <u>show</u>. They were the only <u>creatures</u> that could remain calm in a <u>crisis</u>.

Shaky Ground, page 37

The earthquake <u>hit</u> just before dawn. It <u>came</u> without warning and <u>caught</u> everyone by surprise. Everyone <u>felt</u> the effects immediately. Houses <u>shook</u>, windows <u>rattled</u>, lampposts <u>wobbled</u>, and several telephone poles <u>fell</u> over. Dogs <u>barked</u>, cats <u>screeched</u>, and a few babies <u>screamed</u> at the top of their lungs.

The damage <u>was</u> everywhere. Cracks <u>spread</u> through the streets like spiders' webs. A billboard <u>fell</u> and <u>crushed</u> a parked car. Two trees <u>dropped</u> into giant holes, and only their tops <u>stuck</u> out. In the park, several pipes <u>burst</u> in the fountain, and water <u>poured</u> over the broken benches.

The quake <u>lasted</u> less than a•minute, but it <u>seemed</u> like a lot longer to everyone in the middle of it. After the siren <u>sounded</u> "All Clear!," everyone <u>went</u> outside out of curiosity. As they <u>walked</u> around, they <u>saw</u> the incredible damage. Luckily, there <u>were</u> no serious injuries.

Just in Time, page 38

1. took
2. agreed
3. nodded
4. did
5. were
6. had
7. said
8. caught
9. played
10. shuddered
11. looked
12. got
13. do
14. have

Rescue Mission, page 39

1. am
2. is
3. are
4. Aren't
5. have
6. look
7. were
8. need
9. want
10. needs
11. is
12. am

The Small Print, page 40

1. and
2. because (or since)
3. so
4. but
5. unless
6. if
7. but
8. If
9. while
10. or
11. but

The Bubble Gum Game, page 41

Some answers may vary.

1. because (or since)
2. so
3. but
4. because (or since)
5. either
6. or
7. and
8. but
9. if
10. because (or since)
11. so
12. or

Play Time, page 42

Not all pronouns from the list are used.

1. our
2. you
3. He
4. she
5. She
6. her
7. They
8. them
9. he
10. her
11. you
12. it
13. our

Family Reunion, page 43

Not all pronouns from the list are used.

1. Who
2. them (or us)
3. It
4. me
5. He
6. I
7. you
8. you
9. They
10. you
11. I
12. You
13. he

School Rules, page 44

Note that adverbs also modify adjectives and other adverbs. Answers will vary. These are possibilities.

There are several tricks to doing well in Mr. Stubbs's class. First you must <u>always</u> remember to arrive <u>early</u> every day. When you walk in the door, smile <u>brightly</u>. Otherwise he will <u>casually</u> ask you what is wrong.

During class, you must take notes <u>neatly</u>. If you don't, Mr. Stubbs will ask you very <u>loudly</u> if you already know everything. Answer him <u>nicely</u> and <u>quickly</u> tell him that you like his tie.

When Mr. Stubbs is teaching, you must <u>never</u> yawn. He also does not like it if you cough <u>often</u>, but if you cough <u>quietly</u> he might not care. Whatever you do, don't blow your nose <u>constantly</u>! He <u>really</u> hates that.

Mr. Stubbs uses short sentences that make him sound bossy sometimes. He'll say, "Come <u>here</u>!" or "Go <u>there</u>!" or "Do this <u>now</u>!" You might think he is in a bad mood, but he <u>really</u> does not want to waste any time. You will <u>definitely</u> learn a lot in his class.

Animal Traits, page 45

Answers will vary. These are possibilities.

1. sleepy brown bear
2. giant, slippery whale
3. friendly, magical unicorn
4. old, majestic eagle
5. huge, ferocious tyrannosaurus
6. kind, ancient dragon
7. frisky, young goat
8. energetic, furry puppy
9. hungry, sly shark
10. big, shy moose

Eating Out, page 46

Answers will vary. These are possibilities.

1. diner
2. quiet
3. hungry
4. hot dog
5. plastic
6. paper
7. pudding
8. gooey
9. soda
10. silk

Quick Visit, page 47

Answers will vary. These are possibilities.

1. peasant
2. rags
3. cottage
4. peasant
5. hay
6. peasant
7. whisper
8. young girl
9. cottage
10. peasant
11. stones
12. walked
13. quietly

This Spooky Old House, page 48

Answers will vary. These are possibilities.

1. deserted mansion
2. dim green glow
3. high-pitched scream
4. shrill screaming
5. secret trapdoor
6. a dark shadow
7. quietly
8. gloom
9. limping figure
10. dreadful error

Sense-itivity, page 49

Answers will vary. These are possibilities.

1. sunny/foggy
2. fresh/musty
3. smooth/sticky
4. sweet/salty
5. splash/growl

Second Look, page 50

Answers will vary. These are possibilities.

1. a bashful monkey
2. the generous wolf
3. the bossy king

4. a happy baby
5. the sleepy puppy
6. the rude guest
7. the gentle giant
8. the bold turtle
9. the shiny pail

Running Late, page 51

Unneccessary words are underlined. Answers will vary. These are possibilities.

On the very first day of school, Jennifer was late. She didn't make it to school on time. She was ten years old, but would be eleven on her next birthday. On the way to school, she had been listening to the *Amazon River Rats*, who had sold more than ten million CDs. They are very popular.

Mrs. Wilton, her teacher who taught her math, science, English, and other subjects, was not interested in Jennifer's excuses. She had struggled with her own personal problems that morning after eating her usual daily breakfast of a poached egg on toast. She had gotten stuck in traffic behind several cars: three red cars, two blue cars, and one purple van. One driver, who was driving a purple van, kept honking the horn repeatedly, over and over again.

"If *I* can get here on time, Jennifer," said Mrs. Wilton, checking her ancient watch with the old, worn leather band, "so can you." She had worn that watch every day for twenty years, day in and day out. In fact, this was the very same watch she used to look at anxiously and nervously when she was running late to school as a kid in various grades.

Aches and Pains, page 52

Answers will vary. These are possibilities.

Are you one of the millions of the many Americans living in the United States in houses or apartments who suffer from painful headaches? Have you wished in vain for some kind of temporary relief from the steady pounding that doesn't stop, but just seems to go on and on? If so, then we have news for you if you just keep reading. For just $19.95 in dollars and cents, we will send you our new headache stopper—PainBane. It is not available in any stores, whether or not they're big or small or sell other things. It is available only through this special TV offer you're listening to right now. Act now, and we'll also send you PainGain, which works in just the opposite way. So don't waste another second or minute. Pick up that phone and dial. Operators are standing by with their shoes and socks on, ready to answer your call.

Up a Creek, page 53

Answers will vary. These are possibilities.

We're in trouble now. We would have been fine if you had kept quiet. But, no, you had to tell the secret. That's why I glared at you. I wanted to tell you to go away. But since you're crazy, I'll be happy if you leave me alone. If we're lucky, we will just barely escape. If not, that's life.

Welcome Matt, page 54

1. despised
2. village
3. everybody
4. determine
5. sort
6. stare
7. instructor
8. fortunate
9. sack
10. permanently

Garage Sale, page 55

1. mom
2. her
3. buy
4. under
5. sunny
6. treasure
7. gleaming
8. worthless
9. right
10. night
11. hate

Some Assembly Required, page 56

Answers will vary. These are possibilities.

1. tools
2. machine
3. wires
4. nails
5. sides
6. wheels
7. cover
8. handles
9. lever
10. garbage can